In this poignant dialogue between an artist and her father, Helen Zughaib offers glim[...] lands and generations . . . Like dreaming in color, her visual interpretations render ge[...] at times, melancholy, in vibrant mosaics of memory.

> —Richard Doughty,
> *Aramco World*

Graced by listening to her father tell his stories, Helen Zughaib gathers her core personal experiences to magically carry us into distant places of beauty, joy, devotion and love. Her perfectly patterned visual images create a path of radiance. Father and daughter together in this book will break open your heart.

> —Helen Frederick,
> Professor Emerita, George Mason University School of Art

In *Stories My Father Told Me* . . . Helen Zughaib and her father, Elia, narrate the stories of a people who survive political turmoil and uncertain times with humor, grace, and empathy—all rooted in unconditional love. Zughaib's artistic mastery is on full display in the series, transporting the viewer to a world of beauty and wonder as her father's words are brought to life. *Stories My Father Told Me* reflects the complexities of migration and displacement, as scattered families struggle to keep their bonds intact and memories from fading. Like Jacob Lawrence's *Migration Series,* this timely publication is sure to become a canonical work of Diaspora Studies.

> —Maymanah Farhat,
> Writer and curator

This is a work of true ambassadorship. Helen Zughaib is a born diplomat, who plies her craft through exquisite art and gentle, insightful storytelling. If there were more like her and more like this wonderful book, the world would be far more peaceful, tolerant and loving. *Stories My Father Told Me* arrives at exactly the right moment.

> —Jennifer Heath,
> Editor, *An Echoing Resistance: Art of the Arab Spring and Its Aftermath*

These treasured stories ignite memories of life enriched by tradition and ritual, aroma and flavor—all alive in Helen's brilliant, delicate mosaics.

—Karen Leggett Abouraya,
Author *Hands Around the Library: Protecting Egypt's Treasured Books*

Elia and Helen Zughaib have created a cure for xenophobia. Elia's stories capture our hearts as he tells his daughter about his daily life and folktales in far-away Syria and Lebanon. Helen's signature style, playful patterns, and joyful colors awaken the child in each of us. Once this book is in libraries, schools and homes around the world, readers will begin to understand and love—not fear—the people in far-away lands.

—Delinda Hanley,
Washington Report on Middle East Affairs

This collection of poignant reminiscences by the artist's father of his boyhood in Syria and Lebanon is made sweeter by the paintings she creates to illustrate them. It is a love poem to a lost past and a testament to the bonds of family that this father-and-daughter collaboration beautifully represent.

—Alex Kronemer,
Writer/Director of the Emmy nominated film *The Sultan and the Saint*

In her book, *Stories My Father Told Me: Memories of a Childhood in Syria and Lebanon,* artist Helen Zughaib brings to life colorfully nuanced tales of a time and place preserved in memory. Her charming images depict touchstones of culture with universal resonance—warm family rituals rendered in her signature style, offering the viewer hours of delightful discovery.

—Dagmar Painter
Curator, Gallery Al-Quds, Washington

Stories My Father Told Me

For my incredible parents, Elia and Georgia Zughaib,
who give me continued support and all their love.
And for my wonderful husband, Andy,
who has always been by my side.

—Helen Zughaib

For my grandchildren: Emily, Catherine, and Laithe.

—Elia Zughaib

The stories in this book recount events from Elia
Zughaib's Syrian and Lebanese childhood in the 1930s
and early 1940s, in what are now the Lebanese villages
of Marjayoun, Zahle, and Kfeir. After sharing his stories
in family settings over the years, Elia finally agreed to set
them down in written form at the urging of his daughter,
the artist Helen Zughaib, who contributed the title to
this volume. The accompanying art work was created by
Helen. The result is a collaboration of story and image
by father and daughter, celebrating the richness of Syrian
and Lebanese life and culture in a bygone era.

Stories My Father Told Me

Memories of a Childhood in Syria and Lebanon

Illustrations by Helen Zughaib
Text by Elia Zughaib

حكايات رواها لي أبي:
ذكريات كفولة في سوريا ولبنان

Cune

Stories My Father Told Me:
Memories of a Childhood in Syria and Lebanon
by Helen Zughaib and Elia Zughaib
© 2020 Helen Zughaib and Elia Zughaib
Cune Press, Seattle 2020
First Edition

Hardback   ISBN 9781951082659 $24.00

Catalogue in Publication
Names: Zughaib, Helen, 1959- artist, author. | Zughaib, Elia, 1927-
Title: Stories my father told me : memories of a childhood in Syria and
Lebanon / by Helen Zughaib and Elia Zughaib.
Description: First edition. | Seattle : Cune Press, 2018.
Identifiers: LCCN 2018029846 (print) | LCCN 2018027889 (ebook) | ISBN
9781951082659 (hardback) | ISBN 9781614572299
(eBook) | ISBN 9781614572305 (Kindle)
Subjects: LCSH: Zughaib, Helen, 1959- Stories my father told me. | Tales in
art.
Classification: LCC ND237.Z85 A75 2018 (ebook) | LCC ND237.Z85 (print) | DDC
759.13--dc23
LC record available at https://lccn.loc.gov/2018029846

Author's Note: The medium of the paintings in this book is gouache on board.
Special Thanks: to the Puffin Foundation for their generous grant and to editor Lisa Suhair Majaj, calligrapher Mamoun Sakkal, and publisher Scott C. Davis at Cune Press, who made this book possible and were endlessly patient with me.

Aswat: Voices from a Small Planet (a series from Cune Press)
Looking Both Ways   Pauline Kaldas
Stage Warriors   Sarah Imes Borden
Stories My Father Told Me   Helen Zughaib & Elia Zughaib

Syria Crossroads (a series from Cune Press)
The Plain of Dead Cities   Bruce McLaren
East of the Grand Umayyad   Sami Moubayed
Syria - A Decade of Lost Chances Carsten Wieland
The Road from Damascus   Scott C. Davis
A Pen of Damascus Steel   Ali Ferzat
Leaving Syria   Bill Dienst, MD & Madi Williamson
White Carnations   Musa Rahum Abbas
The Dusk Visitor   Musa Al-Halool

《ⵑ》Cune Cune Press: www.cunepress.com | www.cunepress.net

Contents

Definitions

Here are definitions of a few of the Arabic terms used by Elia in his stories.

argilla	water pipe
eid	feast or feast day
hara	narrow street
jiddu	grandfather
jurn	stone mortar
hallab	milkman
kharjiyyi	spending money
kibbeh	ground meat with crushed wheat and onions
kibbeh nayye	raw kibbeh
kibbeh bil-sayniyyi	kibbeh baked flat in a pan
kroum	plural of karm, a plot of land with fruit trees, typically fig trees or grapevines, or olive trees
mathani	coffee grinder
mendeel	scarf or headscarf
nawbis	musical bands
nigls	small change
sanduk	box
shabab	young men
sabaya	young ladies
subhiyyi:	morning gathering/brunch
teta	grandmother
zalagheet	ululation; song of joy or sorrow
zuwadi	picnic lunch; non-perishable provisions

Telling Me His Stories

ويروي لي حكاياتي ....

ONE EVENING SEVERAL YEARS AGO, my mother and I were in the kitchen of my parents' home in Alexandria, Virginia after a wonderful family dinner when she said, "Someday, we ought to record your father telling his stories." It had been an evening filled with dad sharing stories of his youth and young adulthood in Syria and Lebanon in the 1930s and early 1940s, before he emigrated to the US in 1946. At the time my mother said this, we were thinking of the old-fashioned way of capturing his stories using an audio recorder.

A few weeks later I was approached by a gallery for a solo exhibition. In our conversation, I mentioned the possibility of a themed show centered on my father's true stories of life in Syria and Lebanon and his ultimate arrival in America. I told the gallery that I envisioned a series of paintings based on my father's stories, inspired by the amazing Jacob Lawrence Migration series I had first seen at the Phillip's Collection near my home in Washington.

The gallery loved the idea, but then I had to ask my father for his approval. This turned out to be not so easy. At first, when I met with both my parents and told them of my show and plans for the exhibit, my father refused, explaining to me that these were private family stories and not to be shared with a wider audience. My mother said they would talk it over. About an hour later, my father called and reluctantly agreed to write down his stories for me.

Often I would go to my parents' home and sit at the table with him while he would tell me the new story he was working on. With each one there was a bit more detail, and this further enriched my subsequent paintings. The conversations also allowed a special intimacy to grow between us. I treasure those times.

One day, my father gave me a ride home to my apartment in Foggy Bottom. On the way, we stopped at a local Mediterranean bakery where they sold Syrian cookies called *barazik*. Back in the car, as we shared a cookie, he remembered another story, about playing *basra* in his grandmother's room. "There," I thought. "I have another great story to paint!"

We continued in this way for several years, a story here and a story there, until there were twenty-four. After handing me the twenty-fourth story, my father said that this was the last one.

I hope he will change his mind.

Helen Zughaib

TELLING ME HIS STORIES

Charity & Compassion

WHEN my father narrated the following tale, he prefaced it by saying, "Jiddu, my father, told me this story. And he said to remember it always."

Once there was an Emir who owned a horse so strong and beautiful that it was known all over the land. Other Emirs were envious and tried to buy the horse, but the owner always refused. Selling the horse, he said, would be like selling a member of his family.

One day a crook came to one of the envious Emirs and offered to steal the horse for a price. A bargain was made.

The crook waited by the side of the road where the Emir and the wonderful horse passed each day. When the Emir approached, the crook began to cry and wail. The Emir stopped to inquire why. The crook replied that he was very sick and needed a doctor. The Emir agreed to help take him to a doctor, but the crook said he was too sick to climb up on the horse. The Emir dismounted to help him onto the horse. As soon as the crook was seated in the saddle he took off at a fast gallop.

The Emir called loudly, "Stop and the horse is yours." The crook stopped and returned, knowing that the Emir would never go back on his word. "Do not say you stole this horse," the Emir said. "Say that I gave it to you. Do this so that charity and compassion will not disappear from our community."

CHARITY & COMPASSION

The Transaction

My FATHER, A GOOD GREEK ORTHODOX, had great respect for Tsarist Russia. When the Tsar was defeated and exiled after the Bolshevik Revolution, he assumed that it was a temporary exile. Believing the Tsar and the Russian Empire would soon return to their previous glory, he saw an opportunity to make his fortune.

He sold some of the family possessions, cattle, land, jewelry, and other belongings and bought Russian rubles, which by then had become almost worthless. All the rubles were stacked in wooden boxes and stored in a big closet in Jiddu's house. In the beginning, we children could not touch the rubles, only look at the hoard from a safe distance.

Time passed, the Tsar and his family were killed, and my father's rules were gradually relaxed. We were allowed to handle the rubles, count them, admire their various sizes and denominations, and, in his absence, show them to our friends.

Finally, the rubles lost all their mystique. Even my father would occasionally laugh at his folly, although no one else would have dared to bring up the economic details of that transaction.

THE TRANSACTION

Blind Charity

الحسنة العمياء

ONE DAY MY FATHER AND I were chatting about everything and nothing in particular when he told me that the following day he was going to *Dayr Saydnaya* and that I could accompany him if I wanted to. The *Dayr*, a nunnery in the outskirts of Damascus, was his favorite charity. I accepted gladly, as this was one trip I enjoyed and looked forward to.

We arrived on a sunny afternoon, climbed the stone steps, and entered the courtyard where we sat to rest and reflect. After a time, my father spoke.

"What do you think of charity?" he asked.

"I think that people appreciate good deeds because such acts meet their special needs," I replied.

"What about blind charity," he continued, "where the donor does not know the recipient and has no idea what the need may be?"

I did not have a ready answer, so my father continued. "Blind charity is the most sincere kind of charity," he said. He then recited this line of poetry, *"Wasnaa jamilan walaou fi ghayri mawdi'ihi fala yadiou jamilan aynama sunia."* (Do charitable deeds even if they may be out of place, for no act goes unrewarded.)

He then illustrated his point with the following story.

Once there was a well-to-do woman, the wife of a governor of a prosperous port city, who was known as the woman of jasmine because of the fragrant jasmine she grew in her garden. Once a week she took a large basket and sealed it with tar to make it waterproof. In the bottom of the basket she wrote the line of poetry, *"Wasnaa jamilan . . ."* Then she filled the basket with food, water, and clothing. After this was done, she gave the basket to a fisherman who took it far beyond the breakwater and dropped it into the open sea, to be carried away by the waves and wind.

After some time, the woman of jasmine and her family took a long boat trip to visit relatives in another port city. Heavy storms demolished their boat, and many on board drowned. Thrown into the water, the woman of jasmine

grasped a nearby plank of wood and clung to it. Eventually she drifted to shore where she collapsed with hunger, thirst, and exhaustion.

When the woman of jasmine woke up, she was in a beautiful garden. A finely-dressed lady was sitting next to her. "My servants found you on the beach," the lady told her. "At first, they thought you were dead. When they realized that you were still alive they brought you to my garden and laid you here to recover."

The woman of jasmine was confused and shaken by her traumatic experience. Seeing her predicament, the finely-dressed lady asked her servants to make the woman comfortable and to bring her food and drink. Within a week, the woman of jasmine had regained her strength, but could recall little of her previous life. "No matter," said the lady of the house, "You can stay with us and work as our washer woman while you recover." The woman of jasmine gladly accepted.

The household servants brought the woman of jasmine a large reed basket of laundry to wash. The woman took out the items of clothing one by one. When she reached the bottom of the basket, she saw the line of poetry which she herself once wrote in the bottom of baskets before dropping them into the sea: "*Wasnaa jamilan . . . .*" In shock, she realized that she was looking at a line of poetry written in her own hand. She sat down and began to cry.

When the lady of the house came to check on the laundry, she found the woman of jasmine in tears. Asked why she was crying, the woman of jasmine explained, "This basket was one of my own!" She went on to describe how she would fill such baskets with provisions and drop them into the sea, hoping that shipwrecked people might find the baskets and use the food and water to survive.

The lady of the house was amazed. She told the woman of jasmine that once she and her husband were aboard a ship that sank in a storm. They would have lost their lives but for a large basket that drifted by. They clung to it until they were washed onto a nearby shore. Once on land, they were astonished to find provisions in the basket. They gratefully ate and drank, and when they had revived, they walked to the city. There they found jobs and a place to stay. They survived and, in time, prospered. Out of sentimentality, they kept the basket and used it for their washing, thinking that someday they would learn more about it and about the line of poetry written inside.

Moved, the lady of the house thanked the woman of jasmine for unknowingly saving her life. When the lady's husband returned home and learned of these events, he too was overwhelmed, and insisted that the washer woman live with them as a member of their family.

Gratefully, the woman of jasmine accepted. She asked if she could plant white jasmine in the garden. She and her hosts also decided to prepare baskets to drop into the sea. Every week thereafter the woman of jasmine wrote the line of poetry, "*Wasnaa jamilan . . .*" at the bottom of a basket, and she and her hosts filled it with provisions to be dropped into the open sea.

"Let's hope," they said to each other, "that other people in need will find these baskets, as we did. Find them and survive."

BLIND CHARITY

Planting Olive Trees

THIS IS A STORY that was told to my father by his father. It is a lesson that is taught to children all over the Middle East in one form or another.

Visiting Jiddu and Teta, my grandparents, in their mountain village was always a special treat. Teta would have special sweets and my favorite foods prepared for me. Best of all, though, was Jiddu taking me with him to the fields. Sometimes it was a brief trip to see how the plants were growing. But at other times Jiddu would ask me to be "Jiddu's helper" and assist with small chores. During one visit, Jiddu told me that we would be planting olive trees. Because we would be staying in the olive fields all day, we had to bring with us a *zuwadi* (picnic lunch), water, and other provisions.

The next morning, Jiddu and I set out for the fields much earlier than usual, with a donkey carrying our provisions and small olive plants. We worked hard planting the young olive trees in the furrows Jiddu had dug earlier. My job was to hold the plant straight while Jiddu dug a small hole in the ground for each tree. Then I would ladle some water from the water drum onto each new olive tree.

During our break for lunch, I told Jiddu that next year I would return to help him harvest the olive crop. He smiled and said that would be difficult, because olive trees take many years before they bear fruit. Disappointed, I asked him why we were bothering to plant olive trees if we would be dead before they would give us any fruit. He looked at me with a very serious expression and said, "*Zara'u fa akalna, nazra'u fa ya'kulun.*" They planted so we would eat; we plant so our descendants will eat.

Planting Olive Trees

The Hallab

When I was a small boy I lived in Bab al-Mussalla in Midan, the old quarter of Damascus. I remember being fascinated by the various peddlers who wandered the narrow streets chanting about their products and services. Sellers of fruits, vegetables, and sweets as well as knife sharpeners, pruners, and buyers of old items filled the air with their melodic chants. These rhyming chants never actually mentioned the name of the item being offered, but described in detail its color, freshness, and taste. Buyers knew by the traditional chants what was being offered for sale, which also would dictate the day's menu. The streets were crowded with loaded donkeys, push carts, and peddlers carrying large trays (*sddur*) piled high with cakes and other tasty things.

Children playing in the street or on their way to school would keep an eye out for the sellers of sweets. These were mostly seasonal. Cooked steaming sweet beets and popcorn were sold in winter. Ice with syrup (*sweeq*) was sold in the summer. Breads such as *kaak* and *manaquish* were sold year-round, while *tamari* (a brittle semisweet cookie made with molasses syrup) was sold only on feast days. Invariably a child's daily allowance was exchanged for a *kaak* with *za'atar*, a *tamari*, or a handful of *hanblas* (a small, tasty fruit easy to carry in the pocket). Usually the sweets were shared or bartered with others, thus expanding the purchasing power of the child's allowance.

The nicest of the peddlers was the *hallab* (milkman) who chanted about his fresh milk. The *hallab* had a small flock of eight to ten Damascene goats that accompanied him. The goats were mostly brown, large and gentle, and each had two strands of hair dangling from their necks. Small children would stand eye to eye with the goats to pet and hug them on their way to school. The *hallab* did not mind, and both the goats and the children loved the attention.

The *hallab* carried a pail (*suttle*), a measuring can (*kaylee*), and a long bamboo stick. When a housewife opened her door and asked for milk, the *hallab* would milk one of his goats right then and there. If she planned to make yoghurt that day, more milk would be required. If the goats began to wander, the *hallab* gently guided them back to the herd. After the fresh milk was delivered and the *hallab* was paid he continued on his route, chanting about his beautiful goats.

The other peddlers could not compete with the *hallab*, his wonderful goats, and the pleasure of petting the gentle and loving animals. After powdered milk appeared on the grocery shelves, milk never tasted the same again.

The Hallab

The Show Box

Long before cinemas or television entertained Lebanese and Syrian children, there was *sanduk al-firji*—the show box. *Sanduk al-firji* was a brightly decorated semi-circular box that was strapped to the back of an itinerant entertainer. He would come into the village, loudly chanting previews of the stories he had to offer, and go from *hara* to *hara* (street to street) till he ended up in the village square.

There, he first unstrapped the *sanduk*. It was about eighteen inches high and had five or six glassed portholes equidistant from each other. On either end of the box were two small inner poles attached to a scroll that held bright glossy pictures. The pictures illustrated one or more of the fabled Arab stories, such as *Antar and Abla* or *Abu Zayd al-Hilali*.

He then placed the box on a stool and set up a circular bench facing it. The village children took turns handing him their *kharjiyyi* (spending money). In groups of five or six they peeked into the box and watched the story through the portholes. The entertainer rolled the screen, chanting about the beauty of the ladies, the courage of the men, and the strength of their horses. Usually the lucky viewers would briefly give up their places to siblings or friends who did not have enough *kharjiyyi* to buy a viewing for themselves.

When all those who wanted to see the show had been accommodated, the entertainer strapped the show box to his back, picked up the stool and bench, and walked to the next village, chanting previews to entice new viewers as he went.

It was an amazement to me at the time how he synchronized the chanted story with the pictures on the rolling scroll. And the box, the beautiful *sanduk*, with its colorful pictures and many tiny mirrors, was a source of wonder even without the stories.

THE SHOW BOX

The Performing Bear, the Dancing Monkey & the Dancing Gypsies

الدب والقرد والغجر الراقصون

When I was growing up in Bab Al-Mussala, in the old quarter of Damascus, on rare occasions we would hear the beat of a drum and the intonations of a gypsy chanting, announcing his performing bear and dancing monkey. This was one occasion no child wanted to miss. We children begged and pleaded for a few extra piasters to go see this incredible sight.

We could also hear the jingling of a tambourine and the sing-song of a gypsy who sang and played his tambourine and *bouzouk*. He was accompanied by a young gypsy girl in a colorful, flowered skirt that twirled around as she danced. They went from *hara* to *hara* (street to street) trying to entice new audiences to come to listen to them.

The bear, captive on a strong chain, would obey commands: How does a young bride walk? How does an old man sit? How does an old woman wash laundry? How does a woman knead dough? The monkey, also on a leash, would dance, do tricks, and pretend to be a pick-pocket. At the end of the amazing performance, the tambourine or drum was passed around to collect coins from those who had watched the show. The troubadours then moved on to the next *hara*.

Many times children would follow the gypsies and end up getting lost. One time I got lost and wandered the streets until finally a kindhearted man led me back home where my mother was waiting.

THE PERFORMING BEAR, THE DANCING MONKEY & THE DANCING GYPSIES

Evenings in the Kroum

أمسيات الكروم

EVERY SUMMER I SPENT SEVERAL WEEKS at my grandparents' house in Zahle, a village in the foothills of Mount Sannine, Lebanon. The best part of the visit was the trip Jiddu and I made each year to the nearby *kroum* (orchards and vineyards). We would spend a week working in the *kroum*, talking and just being together.

During the day, Jiddu and I worked in the field. He would tell me what to do and explain to me why things were done in a certain way. Jiddu not only talked to me, he would also talk to the trees and grape vines as if they were people visiting us. In a way, the *kroum* had become intertwined with the family, part of the community. As he worked, Jiddu would tell me that this tree was planted when Uncle Jamil was born, that tree was planted when Aunt Wadi'a was married, this vine was planted when As'ad was baptized. Every place and plant in the vineyard was connected to something. Sometimes the relation was to national or world events, but mostly the connections were to family events. The fields and the *kroum* were a diary of family history which he was passing on to me.

Jiddu was also an authority on the wild plants and herbs which grew in and around the *kroum*. *This plant is good for curing a cold*, he would say. *This is good for an upset stomach; this is good to flavor a stew.* We would collect many of these herbs and wild flowers and dry them to use in winter.

Every evening after supper, Jiddu would light the kerosene lamp, brew some herbal tea over the charcoal fire, and then begin telling stories about our family. He would tell stories about those who had gone abroad, those who did well, and those who did not; the good sheep and the black sheep. And then, if he wasn't tired, Jiddu would recite poetry or tell stories that usually had a moral or lesson to them. He never preached to me, but he always made sure I got the message.

More than anything else, Jiddu loved poetry. He loved to recite poems and he loved to hear poetry being recited. Sometimes he would ask me to recite poems I had learned in school. I tried my best, but I could not satisfy his thirst for hearing one poem after another. Once, when I was about thirteen, he asked me to recite poetry. I could only remember one poem and part of another. When I stopped reciting, he turned the kerosene lamp off and we went to sleep.

The next night he asked me to recite more poetry. I repeated the same poem that I had recited the night before. Jiddu protested that this was the same piece that I had recited the previous evening. And I confessed that it was all I knew. Jiddu looked at me for some time before saying that if after eight years of school all I could remember was a poem and a half, then I was wasting my time and my parent's money, and that I had better quit school and start working!

After that, Jiddu never asked me to recite anything. He continued to tell me stories, and to teach me about the trees and plants. Poetry, however, never re-entered our life in the *kroum*.

EVENINGS IN THE KROUM

Making Kibbeh on Sunday Morning

تكضير الكبّة صباح الآكد

I LOOKED FORWARD ALL YEAR TO SUMMER HOLIDAYS in Zahle with my Jiddu and Teta. One of my most cherished memories of those vacations was the preparation of the Sunday brunch.

Jiddu's house was large, with a big balcony that wrapped around the second story of the house and overlooked the courtyard. I loved to sleep on that balcony. The nights were cool, and in the early morning the birds would sing beautiful and endless songs. Each Saturday night, I looked forward to the next morning with great anticipation, not because of the birds singing but because of the noisy preparation of the Sunday brunch that would start early in the courtyard below the balcony.

Early in the morning, Jiddu or one of my uncles would go to the butcher to get a leg of lamb (*habra*), lamb's liver (*mi'lak*), and tenderloin (*ftili*) to make *kibbeh* and *shish kebab*. The men would begin to prepare the meat while the women pounded the *kibbeh* in the *jurn*. Young girls would begin the lengthy and tedious task of making the *tabbouli*.

As the *shish kebab* roasted over a charcoal fire, small dishes of *kibbeh nayye* would be passed around to eat. Tomatoes and cucumbers, fresh from the garden, would be sliced and set out. Arak was poured into tiny glasses and passed around to drink. Anyone walking by the house would be invited in for arak and a bite to eat. The conversation became more animated as the morning went on.

The brunch progressed slowly. No one had to go to work, and only some of the women went to church. The rest of the family stayed in the courtyard roasting meat, preparing the *tabbouli*, and making the *kibbeh*. Later the women who had gone to church would return to finish preparing the different *kibbeh* dishes. Smaller *kibbeh* balls were stuffed and fried. *Kibbeh* balls as big as grapefruit were broiled over the charcoal fire. *Kibbeh bil-sayniyyi* would be baked in pans in the oven. Throughout the morning, everyone ate, drank, and discussed local, national, and international events. More people would stop by the courtyard to visit.

After the *kibbeh* was done, lunch, which had actually begun early in the morning, was officially served. By then most people were no longer hungry, but every dish would be tasted and compared to those of the previous Sunday, with the *tabbouli* and *mi'lak* usually receiving the highest praise. When no one could eat or talk anymore, everyone went to rest. I too went to the balcony to have a long nap before waking up late in the afternoon to have a cup of coffee and have my fortune read by one of my aunts.

Making Kibbeh on Sunday Morning

Making Raisins & Drying Figs

My sister and I loved to visit Jiddu's and Teta's house in the mountains. We were free to play in the garden, make new friends, and ride on Jiddu's donkey. But the best days were those that we spent in the *kroum*. When we went to the *kroum* to harvest fruits, we had to leave the house very early in the morning because Jiddu insisted that the grapes and figs should be picked while the dew was still on them.

To harvest the figs, Jiddu and I would climb the fig tree, fill our basket with ripe figs, and then lower the basket to Teta and my sister. They then spread the figs on cloth sheets, flattened them, and covered them with a clean cheese cloth to protect them from dust and insects. After about ten days in the hot sun the figs would be dried and ready to be put in storage for the winter.

Making raisins, however, was more complicated. Teta first took the bunches of grapes and laid them neatly on white sheets covered with straw. My sister always wanted the rows of grapes to be separated by color, long neat stripes of purple, black, and white. Teta humored her even though once they were dried they would be all mixed up together. After the grapes were lined up to my sister's satisfaction, Teta continued by dipping bunches of *tayyoun*—herbs that grew wild on the slopes adjacent to the vineyard—into a mixture she had prepared from ashes, water, and other ingredients. She then sprinkled the liquid onto the grapes.

Every day we would return to the vineyards to check on the drying figs and raisins and to moisten the grapes. When it was time to return home, we always left with dried figs, raisins, and new stories to share with our friends in the city.

Making Raisins & Drying Figs

Playing Basra

لعبة الباصرة

I N SYRIA AND LEBANON, *basra* is one of the simplest and easiest card games. Older members of the family teach the younger ones how to play it. When you want the younger kids to quiet down and stay out of trouble and everything else fails, *basra* is the answer.

My Teta was no exception. During inclement weather when we could not play outside, she would propose a *basra* game. Sometimes we would suggest a game ourselves, knowing full well there would be treats after the game.

The game began with Teta sitting on the rug in her room. We completed the circle sitting around her. Usually she dealt the cards, although sometimes, to please us, she would ask one of us to deal instead. We liked playing *basra* with Teta. She overlooked minor cheating and always made sure one of us won.

To us, Teta seemed very old. At the time, we did not know of anyone older. She wore a colorful *mendeel* (headscarf) trimmed with beads wrapped around her head. She also wore several skirts, one over the other, with a bright *maryul* (apron) on top. We were fascinated with the skirts, under which she had a homemade cloth bag, or *dikki*, tied around her waist with a ribbon. In this bag she kept some change and keys.

One key, the most interesting key to us, opened a small wooden cupboard in her room in which she kept cookies and sweets. Another key opened a large enameled wooden box in which she kept her finer things, her valuables, and any large-denomination money.

After the game, we would pester Teta to show us what she had in her cupboard as an indirect way of getting at what was inside. When a request to view the inside of the cupboard did not succeed, a united plea for sweets would be voiced. That demand, uttered in various forms, would ultimately succeed, and sweets would be produced and passed around. If and when the sweets were not in abundance, Teta would distribute small change, or *nigls*, to us.

Playing Basra

Subhiyyi at Teta's House

صبحية عند تيتا

Teta's subhiyyi ritual—a daily morning gathering—was a routine that never varied. We grew up knowing that we, the children, were not to interfere with the morning's activities. Although we enjoyed the ritual and watched the preparations in awe, my grandmother made it clear we were not expected to help.

Six or seven older women, all widowed, would gather at my grandmother's house each morning. In the fall, spring, and summer, the gathering would take place in the courtyard around the water fountain. In the winter the meetings were held in the living room around the charcoal brazier. Two or three *argillas* were prepared, and the flavored tobacco mixed and dampened. I loved the smell of the tobacco being prepared because it was usually mixed with carob or grape molasses. The aroma made me hungry for an *arouss*, a molasses and tahini sandwich.

At about ten o'clock the women would begin to drift in. They did not knock on the door, which was always open anyway. My grandmother would be seated in her usual place, and each woman would sit in her same place. They all dressed in the same way: a black *tannoura* (long skirt) over several slips, with a sash (*dikki*) tied around the waist. On top each woman wore a black jacket over an embroidered vest, with a light blue or grey *mendeel* (scarf) covering her hair. The scarf would be tied coquettishly at an angle, a practice carried over from her younger days.

After the women arrived, usually within minutes of each other, my grandmother would begin the coffee ritual. The coffee beans were placed in the *mahmassi*, a small steel pan with a very long handle so that the hand holding it would not be burned. The slowly roasting beans were stirred with a long-handled spoon until my grandmother determined the color was just right. The beans were spread on a tray to cool, and then one of the women ground them in the *mathani* (the coffee grinder). When my grandmother decided enough ground coffee had accumulated in the little wooden drawer in the *mathani*, she added it to the boiling water in the pot on the brazier and began to stir. When the coffee threatened to boil over, she removed it quickly from the heat, stirred it, and returned it to the fire. This process was repeated three times, and the second time a few teaspoons of sugar were added. The coffee was then served in tiny cups and the conversations began.

What impressed me both at the time and until now was that the stories were always the same, told each time by the same women, and yet the women never seemed to tire of telling or hearing them. They were almost always dated by some important occurrence they all seemed to remember, such as a flood or drought, epidemic or revolution (*tawshi.*) They recalled their birth dates in the same manner, almost always in relation to some calamitous event. My grandmother, for instance, was born during the *tawshi* of 1865. After any of these events were referred to, there was a chorus of "*tinthaker ma tin 'aad*"—*may it be remembered but never repeated.*

Whatever fruits and vegetables were newly in season were announced and commented on as the women took their places. The first crop of any fruit or vegetable was greeted with amazement, as if they had never seen this particular fruit or vegetable before. Sometimes my grandmother brought an especially tedious chore of vegetable preparation to the circle, and the other women shared in the labor. These market announcements and any new gossip, birth, sickness, or trouble with a daughter-in-law were the only additions to the conversation.

Finally, about 1:00 pm, they would rise almost as one and bid my grandmother goodbye until the next day's *subhiyyi.*

SUBHIYYI AT TETA'S HOUSE

Eid Mar Elias

IN SYRIA AND LEBANON, Christian children traditionally celebrate their Saint's Day instead of their birthday. Those who are named Paul (Boulos) for example, celebrate St Paul's Day as their own feast day (*eid*).

Since my name is Elia, my feast day is Mar Elias. When I was a child, the celebration lasted all day. It began when we went to the church named Saint Elias. In the main yard of the church, *nawbis* (musical bands) from surrounding villages would assemble. Sword and *dabki* dancers would arrive. Children, dogs, and beggars thronged the churchyard in large numbers. The young men (*shabab*) would try to impress the young ladies (*sabaya*) with their prowess in foot races, weight lifting, and occasionally horse races.

Those children named after the saint were given new clothes and more than the usual spending money to buy and sample all the treats offered for sale by the various vendors. In the late afternoon, tired and happy, we would return home to wait for friends and relatives to come with more gifts and good wishes.

EID MAR ELIAS

Palm Sunday Procession

موكب أحد الشعنينة

IN CHRISTIAN VILLAGES IN LEBANON, Palm Sunday was a very special day for parents and children alike. Girls wore colorful new dresses and boys had new suits. In many instances, these were the new clothes for the year.

A procession of church members—fathers, uncles, grandfathers—assembled in the back of the church and proceeded up the aisles, accompanied by children holding candles as long as the child was tall. Young children were usually carried by their fathers or older relatives. The whole experience—the music, prayers, incense, new clothes, the special sweets, and the big dinner waiting at home—was memorable.

At the end of the service, people gathered in the courtyard for mutual admiration and *ismallahs* (blessings), vowing to return a year later with an even longer candle and a taller, healthier child.

PALM SUNDAY PROCESSION

Eid Al Salib—Feast of the Cross

AFTER CONVERTING TO CHRISTIANITY, Saint Helena, the mother of Emperor Constantine, went on a pilgrimage to Jerusalem to search for the cross used in the Crucifixion. She stationed groups of believers on all the hilltops between Constantinople and Jerusalem. When she found the cross, she lit a bonfire as a signal, which was then passed to Constantine with bonfires on all the hills.

On the night of the Feast of the Cross in Lebanon, huge bonfires would illuminate the villages as far as the eye could see. There would be intense competitions to see who would have the largest fire. Unguarded piles of hoarded wood could mysteriously disappear and be used to enhance someone else's fire.

After the bonfires had died down and most people had gone home, a few young men and boys would linger, daring each other to jump over the hot ash and embers. Younger or timid boys skipped around the edges, vowing that the next year they would jump over the fire at its widest point.

Eid Al Salib—Feast of the Cross

The Wedding

IN TRADITIONAL WEDDINGS, after the ceremony in the village church the bridal procession proceeds to the groom's house, accompanied by musicians, dancers, relatives, wedding guests, and any available children. Before the bride enters her new home, her mother and mother-in-law perform a ritual which has been repeated for as long as people can remember.

The bride's mother attempts to stick a specially prepared roll of bread dough (*khamiri*) to the upper part of the main doorway. If the dough sticks to the stone arch, the bride's female relatives sing the congratulatory *zalagheet*, for the sticking of the *khamiri* means that the marriage will last.

The mother-in-law then places a ripe pomegranate on the doorstep. The bride must stomp on it with enough force to break the fruit and scatter the seeds, staining her white dress and shoes in the process. If done successfully, the marriage will be fruitful, with many children and grandchildren blessing the house.

After this ritual the festivities begin, usually in the garden. The musicians play their ouds and *dirbakkis* (drums), singers sing, dancers dance, and everyone joins in the wedding feast until late in the evening.

THE WEDDING

A Walk to the Water Fountain

IN THE OLD DAYS, the only water supply for the village was the communal water fountain. Young women (*sabaya*) walked to the fountain at sunset, balancing large colorful water jugs (*jarra*) on their heads. This walk to get water became, over time, a much-anticipated social event known as *mishwar el'ayn*—a walk to the water fountain.

At the fountain, the *sabaya* would show off their fine dresses, chat, and gossip. The young men of the village (*shabab*) would go to the fountain at the same time to watch and innocently flirt with the young women. Occasionally a young man or woman would muster enough courage to say a word or two to a special person.

The *mishwar* stayed as an accepted custom even after people had running water in their homes. The young people in the village would take walks in the late afternoon whether they needed to go to the fountain or not. The *sabaya* and *shabab* would meet, admire each other, and flirt from a safe distance.

A Walk to the Water Fountain

Making Molasses

B Y OCTOBER THE GRAPES had ripened and were ready to be harvested, soon to be made into raisins and molasses. Making molasses was a wonderful three-day ritual involving the whole village of Kfeir. Even the village school closed so that the children could help in harvesting the grapes.

After being harvested, the grapes were packed in wooden crates to be taken to the communal molasses-making site on the edge of Kfeir. There, the women of the village would crush the grapes and strain the juice. The juice was then poured into several huge vats to boil over wood fires. The women would keep the fire burning with firewood collected days in advance. The grape juice would boil, getting thicker by the hour, and the women would stir and stir it, skimming the *raghwi* (foam) from the boiling juice. Best of all, they would ladle out some *raghwi* and some of the thickened grape juice as a treat for the many children eager for a taste. At lunch time, children would bring potatoes and chestnuts to roast in the hot ashes. For those children who did not bring any, there were always extra potatoes and chestnuts to share.

The event was one big happy mess: men carrying grapes, women and children crushing the grapes, fires being stoked, with warnings to children to keep away from the boiling liquid and open flames, potatoes and chestnuts being roasted, and children and chickens running all over the place.

After several days, the molasses would be finished. Each family in the village then received enough molasses to last through the winter, whether or not the family had contributed to the molasses making. Interestingly, no money was ever exchanged and no one measured how much each family contributed or who had worked hardest. This was truly a communal event in which every family in the village shared.

Making Molasses

When a Child is Born
in a Syrian/Lebanese Village

IN SYRIA AND IN LEBANON, THE BIRTH OF A CHILD is a cause for celebration in which members of the family, neighbors and friends all participate. Some traditional practices are still followed today.

In the pas children were born at home with a midwife assisting. A home birth was an occasion on which the female members of the family took active part. They helped the midwife by encouraging the mother-to-be to bite on a handkerchief to stop her screaming *Ya Adra!* (Oh Virgin Mary!), by telling her *sa'adi waladik* (help your child, implying *push!*)—and by making coffee, tea, and drinks of *zhurat* (dried wild aromatic flowers) and *yansoon* (anise) for the visitors who flocked in to participate or just to satisfy their curiosity.

As soon as the child was born, the midwife completed her professional duties by informing the father and other menfolk of the successful birth and of the sex of the child. This was the moment to pay and tip the midwife. The size of the gratuity depended on the sex of the child and whether the family had desired a boy or girl.

After the midwife had gone, the new mother was dressed in a fancy silk bed jacket and the baby was wrapped like a papoose in fancy swaddling clothes. The new father then entered the room and, depending on his financial circumstances, put a piece of jewelry on the mother's pillow and one or more gold coins in the baby's crib.

From the mother's bedroom, the *zalagheet* would begin, led by the grandmother. The joyful ululations continued until all the neighbors and family had joined in.

For forty days the mother would stay in bed, pampered and served, changing silk jackets as often as her husband's wealth permitted. Neighbors, family, and friends dropped in to congratulate the parents, to give unsolicited advice, and to gossip.

During this time, guests were treated to a dish called *mughli*, a mix of spices, powdered rice, and sugar. As the infant grew, *mughli* was followed by *snaniyyi*, served when the baby gets its first tooth. *Snaniyyi* is made from boiled wheat, sugar, sweetmeats, and brightly colored candy. It is piled high on a large tray and sprinkled with *maward* (flower water), *mazahar* (rosewater), and flowers. It is beautiful to look at as well as to eat.

To protect against the evil eye and other misfortunes, blue beads, small icons, and "Hijabs" are pinned to the clothes and baby's crib. Blue beads and Hands of Fatima protect against the evil eye, while Hijabs, amulets, and talismans protect the child from illness, microbes, and other calamities. The Hijab, a small triangular sewn package, conceals a talisman or written prayer with spiritual powers to protect the child. When the child gets older, the Hijab can be sewn into the inner shirt to keep the protective powers working. The Hijab is never to be opened or disrespected in any way.

When a Child is Born in a Syrian/Lebanese Village

Critiquing the Bride—Nakd Al-'Arous

نقد العروس

IN CHRISTIAN LEBANESE VILLAGES, *Nakd Al-'Arous,* or the critiquing of the bride, is a well-known, though vanishing, ritual. It starts when the mother, aunts, and friends of a potential groom start searching for a suitable bride for the young man in question. By word of mouth they hear about marriageable young ladies. Then the mother of the groom-to-be begins to inquire about the recommended girls. Some of the young ladies are eliminated out of hand, while others require the traditional visit. The mother of the girl to be critiqued is notified that the mother of the potential groom and her entourage will be paying a visit to the prospective bride's house.

My sister, a very attractive young lady, received the attention of plenty of suitors. The mother of one such young man, whom my mother did not know, requested a visit through mutual friends. The purpose of the call was made clear from the beginning, thus preventing any misunderstandings.

Mother replied that my sister at age fifteen was too young and still in school and was not interested in marrying anyone at that time. The mother of the potential groom assumed that this attitude was hard bargaining or modesty and did not back down. She may have thought that once the introductions were made, the reluctance of the parents of the bride-to-be would be ameliorated, if not erased altogether. Mother, out of politeness, said if they still wanted to visit they would be welcome. She stressed, however, that she could not speak for my sister nor could she provide any encouragement. A date was set and the time of 4:00 pm chosen, as my sister would be home from school.

Under normal circumstances, the prospective bride would wear her Sunday best, greet the visitors, make coffee, and offer sweets. A day or two before the meeting, my mother told my sister what to expect and the purpose of the call, and asked her to be "presentable" for politeness sake. My sister reacted with shock and told my mother that marriage was the last thing on her mind, and that she wanted to finish high school and planned on college after that. She said she would not be home for the visit.

The day and hour agreed upon arrived but my sister was nowhere to be found. My mother greeted the callers, whom she had never met before. Stiff and belabored conversation ensued. After realizing my sister would not appear, mother again stressed her disapproval of the whole procedure. Irritated and unwilling to accept the rejection of their marriage proposal, the woman redoubled her efforts and attributed mother's reluctance to modesty. Mother finally made the coffee and offered it along with the usual sweets to the guests, who after a decent interval excused themselves and said their goodbyes.

A few minutes after the departure of the visitors, my sister appeared, looking like a white apparition. Her hair, eyebrows, face, and dress were full of flour. Trying to control her laughter, mother asked my sister what had happened, and told her to go clean up and change her dress. My sister explained that when she came home from school, she wanted to escape the whole ordeal, so she climbed the mulberry tree and sat there for a while until she got tired of sitting on the branch. She also suspected that the neighbors might question her sanity, as mulberries were not in season and she was up in the tree for so long. She then climbed down and hid behind the big flour vat, where she remained until the visit was over. As a result, she became covered with flour. My mother asked her again to clean up and she finally did so, but only after eating most of the sweets intended for the guests.

CRITIQUING THE BRIDE—NAKD AL-'AROUS

Reading the Coffee Cup

قــراءة الفنجان

MY AUNT, UM JOSEPH, was known for her ability to see the future by "reading the cup." When the Arabic coffee was finished, the liquid and sediment left were swished around a bit and the cup turned over on the saucer and left to dry for a few minutes. Um Joseph would study the patterns that were left in the cup, turning it slowly little by little, and would then make her predictions for the next year.

She had a patio, or *mustaba*, by a big mulberry tree that separated the house from the vineyard. There she kept a glowing brazier, pots of coffee, hot water, and a stack of cups and saucers. In good weather her patio would always be filled with guests and family sipping coffee and waiting to hear what their futures held in store for them. Occasionally, someone would even bring a turned cup from their own home that had been saved because it had intriguing and unusual signs that needed Um Joseph's interpretation.

The guests could be divided into two groups, the believers and the doubters. For a long time, I was a doubter. One afternoon my aunt looked at my cup and told me I would take a trip that very day. When I got home my older sister said she had to leave Zahle and go to Beirut and I must accompany her. When I returned, I went straight to Um Joseph to tell her prediction had come true. She was not surprised at all.

I became a believer.

I asked her to show me how to read a cup. Starting at the handle, turning it slowly counter-clockwise until you reach the other side of the handle, that is a year. She showed me the signs for trips, happy or sad gatherings, enemies (snakes), incoming gifts, and good news. She said if the cup sticks to the saucer, that means the coffee drinker is in love. She said you must know your guests, listen to all their news, and have a *tim daffy*, a warm mouth. In other words, always say something nice.

Now when I amuse family and friends by reading their cups, I always remember Um Joseph's dicta: Know your guests, listen to everything being said, and keep a *tim daffy*.

READING THE COFFEE CUP

Crossing the Litani

IN 1940-41, the British forces in Palestine attacked the Vichy French forces in Lebanon and Syria. One of the invasion routes went through Jdeidet Marjayoun, where I was staying with my mother and sisters. Everyone in the village decided to leave before the arrival of the troops.

Clusters of people assembled in some disorder and began walking toward the Litani River. Those who had brought *zuwadi* (non-perishable foods) shared their provisions. Had it not been for the sound of artillery shells bursting in the distance, the whole event could have been described as a slowly moving picnic. They reached the river and waited for morning in order to cross.

In the morning, my mother realized she had fled without any documents. She would not proceed without them, and sent me back to get them. The trip was uneventful except for the stragglers who kept asking me why I was going in the wrong direction. At home I found the steel tube where my mother kept the papers (birth certificates, identification documents, school diplomas, etc.), locked the house, and began the long walk back to the river.

When I reached my family, most of the others had already crossed the river. My mother had refused to leave without me. But then she admitted to another reason for not going: her intense fear of riding a horse across. There were no alternatives. The river was deep and wide, the current was fast, and the fighting was getting closer. Three men and a horse were hired, one man to lead the horse and the other two to hold my mother on the horse. The crossing was safe but noisy, with my mother screaming and waving the metal tube with the papers all the way to the other bank.

The owners of the horse, although their fee was doubled, vowed never to help another heavy and hysterical woman to cross the river.

CROSSING THE LITANI

Saying Goodbye

AFTER A VERY LONG WAIT, permission to travel to America had been granted, reservations on a ship from Beirut to New York City had been made, and a departure date became certain. The goodbyes began in the village. Relatives, friends, and neighbors came to drink coffee with us, exchange stories about others who had emigrated, and wish us well for the journey.

Finally, two days before the actual departure, the entire family traveled to Beirut where we stayed in a hotel and said the final goodbyes. My mother could not believe that she was finally emigrating with her family to America. She put all the passports, tickets, and whatever jewelry and money she had into a special handbag which she held onto even in her sleep.

She also had to be certain that the suitcases packed with gifts for her sisters in America were safe. A large Oriental rug, purchased as a gift from Damascus for her sister Julia, was wrapped separately and always kept in her sight. Hotel employees, relatives, and especially me were fully occupied with guard duty for two days.

On the morning of the departure it was determined that the ship was too big to come to the pier in the port. Passengers, suitcases, last minute gifts, and the carpet had to be put into a large rowboat manned by four sailors. My mother insisted on sitting on the rug no matter what that did to the stability of the boat. When everything was safely on the big ship, she demanded that the sailors put all the suitcases, as well as the carpet, in her cabin. They argued that everything not needed on the voyage must be put in the hold. It took an officer of the ship to intervene and guarantee that nothing would be stolen.

My daughter now has that carpet in her dining room.

SAYING GOODBYE

Coming to America

IT WAS THE END of a long sea voyage. During dinner on the boat the night before we arrived, we learned that our ship, the Vulcania, would be passing by the Statue of Liberty at about 4:00 am the next morning. A spontaneous decision was made by some of the younger passengers to see the Statue of Liberty.

And so, sixteen days after leaving the port of Beirut for New York City, an exuberant group of young people from Syria, Lebanon, and Palestine stayed up all night to greet the dawn and the Statue of Liberty.

I remember it was a clear morning.

Coming to America

Aswat: Voices from a Small Planet

Stories My Father Told Me is part of a new series from Cune Press that features authors writing from their own experience. Aswat (Arabic for "voices") provides a space for voices that are honest, questioning, contemplative, and courageous: voices that narrate lives, challenge boundaries, map new geographies and remap old ones. We have a special focus on writers with a connection to the Middle East, Asia, and Africa.

Aswat Series Editor

The series editor Lisa Suhair Majaj (1960) is a Palestinian-American poet, writer, and scholar. Born in Hawarden Iowa, Majaj was raised in Jordan. She earned a BA in English literature from American University of Beirut and an MA in English Literature, an MA in American Culture, and a PhD in American Culture from the University of Michigan.

Her poetry and essays have been widely published. She has also co-edited three volumes of critical essays on international women writers. *Intersections: Gender, Nation, and Community in Arab Women's Novels* (with Paula Sunderman and Therese Saliba); *Going Global: The Transnational Reception of Third World Women Writers* (with Amal Amireh), and *Etel Adnan: Critical Essays on the Arab-American Writer and Artist* (with Amal Amireh).

In 2008, she was awarded the Del Sol Press Annual Poetry Prize for her book *Geographies of Light*.

Callligrapher

Dr Mamoun Sakkal created the book and chapter titles in *Stories My Father Told Me* using the Arabic font Bustan. An Aleppo native who now lives near Seattle, Sakkal is a graphic artist and typeface designer who has won international competitions for his Arabic calligraphy and type design work. He specializes in fine art that incorporates Arabic typography and geometric design inspired by Arab history. As Cune Press Co-Founder and Art Director, Sakkal also designed the Aswat logo and other logos used by Cune Press.

For more: www.sakkal.com

Cune Cune Press: www.cunepress.com | www.cunepress.net

Cune Press was founded in 1994 to publish thoughtful writing of public importance. Our name is derived from "cuneiform." (In Latin *cuni* means "wedge.")

In the ancient Near East the development of cuneiform script—simpler and more adaptable than hieroglyphics—enabled a large class of merchants and landowners to become literate. Clay tablets inscribed with wedge-shaped stylus marks made possible a broad intermeshing of individual efforts in trade and commerce.

Cuneiform enabled scholarship to exist and art to flower, and created what historians define as the world's first civilization. When the Phoenicians developed their sound-based alphabet, they expressed it in cuneiform.

The idea of Cune Press is the democratization of learning, the faith that rarefied ideas, pulled from dusty pedestals and displayed in the streets, can transform the lives of ordinary people. And it is the conviction that ordinary people, trusted with the most precious gifts of civilization, will give our culture elasticity and depth—a necessity if we are to survive in a time of rapid change.

Aswat: Voices from a Small Planet (a series from Cune Press)

Looking Both Ways	Pauline Kaldas
Stage Warriors	Sarah Imes Borden
Stories My Father Told Me	Helen Zughaib & Elia Zughaib

Syria Crossroads (a series from Cune Press)

Leaving Syria	Bill Dienst & Madi Williamson
Visit the Old City of Aleppo	Khaldoun Fansa
The Plain of Dead Cities	Bruce McLaren
Steel & Silk	Sami Moubayed
Syria - A Decade of Lost Chances	Carsten Wieland
The Road from Damascus	Scott C. Davis
A Pen of Damascus Steel	Ali Ferzat
White Carnations	Musa Rahum Abbas

Bridge Between the Cultures (a series from Cune Press)

Empower a Refugee	Patricia Martin Holt
Biblical Time Out of Mind	Tom Gage, James A. Freeman
Turning Fear Into Power	Linda Sartor
The Other Side of the Wall	Richard Hardigan
A Year at the Edge of the Jungle	Frederic Hunter
Curse of the Achille Lauro	Reem al-Nimer

© Basil Kiwan

Elia Zughaib

Elia Zughaib was born in 1927 in Damascus, and grew up in Syria and Lebanon before coming to America in 1946 to study at Syracuse University. He received his PhD in Political Science from the Maxwell School of Citizenship and Public Affairs and joined the United States Foreign Service in 1959. He served in Lebanon, Iraq, Kuwait, and France until his retirement in 1978 brought him back to Alexandria, Va where he lives with his wife, Georgia.

Photos
Elia Zughaib as a young man in Lebanon and today in the US.
Helen Zughaib in Washington. © Basil Kiwan

Helen Zughaib

Helen Zughaib was born in 1959 in Beirut, Lebanon, where her father was posted as a diplomat. She lived in the Middle East and Europe before coming to the US in 1978 to study at Syracuse University, where she received her BFA from the School of Visual and Performing Arts. Helen's work has been widely exhibited in the US and abroad. Her paintings can be found in private and public collections, including the White House, Library of Congress, World Bank, the US Embassy in Iraq, and the Arab American National Museum in Detroit.

Helen Zughaib lives in Washington with her husband Andy and their cats.